How Did YouTube Start?

An Incredible Journey of the World's Most Influential Video Platform

Joe E. Grayson

Copyright © 2025 Joe E. Grayson, All rights reserved.

No part of this publication may be reproduced, distributed, or transmitted in any form or by any means, including photocopying, recording, or other electronic or mechanical methods, without the prior written permission of the publisher, except in the case of brief quotations embodied in critical reviews and certain other noncommercial uses permitted by copyright law.

Table of Contents

Table of Contents..2
Introduction...3
Chapter 1: The Genesis of an Idea...............................6
Chapter 2: Humble Beginnings................................. 12
Chapter 3: The Viral Spark...19
Chapter 4: The Google Acquisition...........................26
Chapter 5: Building a Platform for Everyone...........33
Chapter 6: The Global Phenomenon........................40
Chapter 7: Shaping Media and History....................47
Chapter 8: The Cultural Zeitgeist.............................. 55
Chapter 9: Challenges and Controversies............... 63
Chapter 10: YouTube Today and Tomorrow............. 68
Conclusion.. 73

Introduction

For decades, the way people consumed videos was a reflection of technological advancements and societal trends. It began with the bulky and fragile VHS tapes, which dominated the home entertainment landscape in the late 20th century. Families would gather around their televisions to watch rented movies or cherished home recordings, rewinding and fast-forwarding their way through hours of analog footage. The arrival of DVDs in the late 1990s brought a sleeker, more durable format, offering better picture quality and interactive menus. This marked a leap forward in how viewers engaged with video content, yet it was still tethered to physical media and limited accessibility.

The dawn of the internet age brought with it a wave of transformation. Cable networks introduced on-demand programming, a precursor to the streaming revolution, allowing audiences to watch their favorite shows at their convenience. But it was the emergence of YouTube in 2005 that truly shattered the boundaries of traditional video consumption. No longer confined to physical media or curated television schedules, YouTube empowered anyone with an internet connection to watch, share, and even create their own content. What began as a simple idea—a platform to share videos—quickly grew into a cultural and technological phenomenon.

YouTube became more than just a website; it was a revolutionary platform that reshaped global communication and entertainment. It provided a space for diverse voices, enabling creators from every corner of the world to share their stories, talents, and ideas. From educational tutorials to viral videos, from live-streamed events to political movements, YouTube became a mirror reflecting the world's diversity and dynamism. Its influence seeped into every aspect of life, from individual hobbies to major cultural shifts, altering the way people consume, share, and interact with media.

This book aims to uncover the incredible journey of YouTube, tracing its path from a modest idea conceived by three former PayPal employees to its current status as the world's most influential video platform. By exploring its origins, growth, and transformative impact, we will dive into the heart of a story that changed the landscape of media forever. Through this narrative, we will uncover how a simple concept revolutionized not only entertainment but also the way humanity connects and communicates.

Chapter 1: The Genesis of an Idea

The story of YouTube begins with three innovative minds who crossed paths while working at a company that was itself a trailblazer in digital transactions: PayPal. Chad Hurley, Steve Chen, and Jawed Karim were part of the team at PayPal during its early days, a time when the company was revolutionizing how people sent and received money online. Each brought unique skills and perspectives to the table, forming a bond that would later catalyze one of the most significant technological innovations of the modern era.

Chad Hurley, a design enthusiast with a knack for visual storytelling, played a pivotal role in PayPal's branding. He was the creative force behind the company's logo, showcasing his ability to blend artistry with technology. Steve Chen, a skilled engineer, was deeply immersed in the technical aspects of building systems that could handle massive volumes of data efficiently. Jawed Karim, another brilliant technologist, was known for his analytical mind and interest in solving real-world problems through technology.

At PayPal, they were part of a dynamic environment fueled by the dot-com boom of the late 1990s and early 2000s. The company's culture encouraged risk-taking, collaboration, and innovation, traits that left a lasting impression on all three. It was a place where big ideas were encouraged and where employees often dreamed of creating something groundbreaking of their own. For Hurley, Chen, and Karim, it was also a place where they forged a partnership that would transcend their work at PayPal.

The trio often engaged in discussions about technology and the internet's potential to reshape human interactions. They shared an entrepreneurial spirit and a desire to create something impactful, something that could solve a problem or fill a gap in the digital world. These informal conversations, combined with their diverse skill sets, laid the groundwork for their eventual collaboration on YouTube.

Their time at PayPal not only honed their skills but also exposed them to the realities of building a successful tech company from the ground up. It taught them the importance of scalability, user-centric design, and the power of a clear vision. These lessons would prove invaluable when they embarked on their journey to create a platform that would forever alter the landscape of media and communication.

After their time at PayPal, Chad Hurley, Steve Chen, and Jawed Karim found themselves brainstorming ideas for a new venture. The internet was evolving rapidly, and they were eager to tap into its transformative potential. Among the many concepts they considered, one stood out—a video-based dating platform. They named it "TuneIn Hookup," envisioning it as a space where users could upload videos of themselves introducing their personalities and interests in hopes of finding a romantic connection.

The idea was unique for its time. While online dating platforms were already gaining traction, most relied solely on static profiles and text-based communication. Adding a video element promised to bring a more personal and engaging touch to the experience, allowing users to showcase their charm, humor, and charisma in ways that text and photos couldn't convey. It was an ambitious idea, born from their belief in the growing importance of video content on the web.

Despite their enthusiasm, the initial concept faced significant hurdles. For one, the technology to support seamless video uploads and streaming was still in its infancy. Bandwidth limitations and inconsistent internet speeds made the user experience cumbersome. Additionally, the public wasn't quite ready to embrace the idea of sharing personal videos online, especially in the context of dating. The awkwardness and hesitance surrounding the concept resulted in a lukewarm reception during early tests.

The challenges forced the trio to rethink their approach. During this time, Jawed Karim encountered a personal frustration that would lead to their breakthrough. He noticed how difficult it was to find specific video clips online, such as Janet Jackson's infamous wardrobe malfunction during the Super Bowl halftime show. The lack of a centralized platform for easily sharing and accessing video content struck him as a glaring gap in the digital ecosystem.

This realization became the turning point. Rather than focusing on dating, they decided to pivot toward a broader video-sharing platform where users could upload and share videos of any kind. The shift was driven by a simple but powerful idea: people wanted an easy way to share moments and stories with the world. By removing the niche focus on dating, they opened the door to limitless possibilities for user-generated content.

With this new direction, they rebranded the project, abandoning "TuneIn Hookup" and laying the foundation for what would soon become YouTube. The pivot wasn't just a change in strategy—it was the spark that would ignite a global phenomenon, setting the stage for a platform that would revolutionize media and communication forever.

Chapter 2: Humble Beginnings

The journey of YouTube officially began on February 14, 2005, in an unassuming location—a small office above a pizza shop in San Mateo, California. The founders, Chad Hurley, Steve Chen, and Jawed Karim, had little more than their vision, their collective skills, and a determination to create something extraordinary. It was a humble beginning, marked by a mixture of ambition and uncertainty, but one that carried the seeds of a revolutionary idea.

The trio worked tirelessly, combining Hurley's design expertise, Chen's engineering skills, and Karim's keen eye for user experience to build the foundation of the platform. They envisioned a site where people could easily upload, share, and watch videos without the technical barriers that had plagued earlier attempts at video sharing. The idea was deceptively simple: create a user-friendly platform that empowered individuals to share their stories with the world.

In those early days, resources were limited, and the workspace was far from glamorous. Yet, the small office above the pizza shop became a hub of creativity and innovation. It was there that the founders developed the core features of YouTube, focusing on simplicity and accessibility. They designed a streamlined process for uploading videos, ensuring that even users with minimal technical knowledge could participate. This emphasis on ease of use would become one of YouTube's defining characteristics.

One of their key breakthroughs was the decision to use Adobe Flash Player to embed videos directly on the site. This allowed users to watch videos instantly within their web browsers, a significant advantage over requiring external software or lengthy downloads. It was a technical solution that bridged the gap between content creators and their audiences, removing friction and making video sharing more intuitive than ever before.

Though the platform was in its infancy, the founders were confident in its potential. They knew that if they could make it simple and appealing, it could attract users from all walks of life. The idea wasn't just about technology—it was about creating a community, a space where anyone could express themselves, connect with others, and leave their mark on the digital world.

In that modest office space above a pizza shop, the foundations of YouTube were laid. It was the birthplace of a platform that would grow far beyond its creators' wildest dreams, transforming not only the internet but also the way humanity shares and consumes information. What started as a small experiment would soon become a global cultural and technological phenomenon.

The first milestone in YouTube's journey came on April 23, 2005, when Jawed Karim uploaded a video titled *"Me at the Zoo."* This 19-second clip, shot at the San Diego Zoo, featured Karim casually standing in front of elephants, sharing a lighthearted observation about their trunks. It was a simple, unpolished video—far from the high-production content that would later dominate the platform—but it carried a profound significance. This inaugural upload was not just the beginning of YouTube's vast video archive; it also symbolized the essence of what the platform was designed to be: a space for personal expression and storytelling.

The unassuming nature of *"Me at the Zoo"* reflected the accessibility that YouTube promised. Anyone, regardless of resources or expertise, could create and share videos with a global audience. This democratic approach was a stark contrast to the tightly controlled and professionalized media outlets of the time, and it resonated with users who were eager to share their own perspectives.

Despite this promising start, YouTube faced significant challenges in its early days. Attracting users to a fledgling platform was no easy task. The internet was still relatively new for many, and the concept of uploading personal videos to a public site was unfamiliar and, for some, intimidating. The founders grappled with how to persuade people to adopt this new form of communication and interaction.

One of the pivotal challenges was encouraging people to create and upload videos. The success of the platform hinged on user-generated content, but in the beginning, there was little incentive for individuals to participate. To address this, the founders actively sought out content, even creating fake accounts and uploading their own videos to simulate activity on the site. This strategy helped populate the platform and gave new users examples of what they could do.

Another turning point came when the team introduced features that made video sharing seamless and appealing. The ability to easily embed YouTube videos on other websites and share them through email links created a ripple effect, exposing the platform to audiences who might not have visited it directly. This functionality was critical in establishing YouTube as a social and viral phenomenon.

Word of mouth also played a key role in YouTube's early traction. Users who discovered the platform began sharing it with friends and family, and before long, its reputation as a fun, innovative space for videos started to grow. Pivotal moments of user engagement—like the first viral videos—cemented its appeal. These early successes demonstrated that YouTube wasn't just a repository for videos; it was a vibrant community where creativity and connection flourished.

From *"Me at the Zoo"* to the first sparks of user engagement, YouTube's early journey was marked by both challenges and ingenuity. The platform's ability to overcome these obstacles and capture the imagination of its users set the stage for its meteoric rise, proving that sometimes, even the simplest beginnings can lead to extraordinary outcomes.

Chapter 3: The Viral Spark

The trajectory of YouTube took a significant leap forward in September 2005, when it hosted its first viral video: a Nike advertisement featuring Brazilian soccer star Ronaldinho. The video showcased Ronaldinho receiving a pair of golden Nike boots, then proceeding to perform a series of awe-inspiring tricks with effortless precision. The highlight of the clip—his repeated volleys that seemingly bounced off the crossbar and back to him without touching the ground—left viewers in awe, sparking debates about its authenticity and amplifying its shareability.

This video was a watershed moment for YouTube. It demonstrated the platform's potential as a marketing tool and its capacity to captivate audiences on a global scale. For Nike, it was a masterstroke, positioning the brand at the forefront of digital innovation while leveraging Ronaldinho's global fanbase. The video resonated with soccer enthusiasts and casual viewers alike, drawing millions of views in a short span—an unprecedented feat for online content at the time.

The success of this video had a profound impact on YouTube's visibility. It brought a surge of traffic to the platform, introducing it to users who might otherwise have never discovered it. For the first time, companies began to recognize YouTube's potential as more than just a platform for personal video sharing. It could be a powerful medium for branding, advertising, and reaching audiences in ways traditional media couldn't match.

The viral nature of the Ronaldinho video also highlighted the social dynamics that would define YouTube's growth. Users weren't just watching videos—they were actively sharing them, discussing them, and embedding them in other websites. The ease of sharing created a ripple effect, spreading the video far beyond the confines of the platform and pulling new users into YouTube's ecosystem.

More importantly, this moment validated the vision of YouTube's founders. The platform's simplicity, accessibility, and focus on user-generated content allowed it to host and amplify videos that resonated with a global audience. It proved that YouTube wasn't just a repository for personal clips; it was a stage for creativity, entertainment, and cultural moments that could transcend boundaries.

The Ronaldinho Nike ad became a symbol of YouTube's emerging identity—a place where the extraordinary could happen, where anyone could share something remarkable and have it seen by the world. This first viral sensation set the tone for the platform's future, laying the groundwork for the countless viral videos that would follow and establishing YouTube as the go-to destination for online video content.

In its earliest days, YouTube's success depended on its ability to attract users and establish itself as a platform for sharing and discovering videos. It didn't take long for both individuals and forward-thinking companies to recognize its immense potential as a promotional tool. The simplicity of uploading videos and the platform's growing audience created a fertile ground for creativity, marketing, and engagement that was unparalleled at the time.

Early users of YouTube were drawn to the platform's user-friendly interface and the unique opportunity it provided for self-expression. For individuals, it was a place to share personal moments, showcase talents, or simply connect with others. From amateur musicians uploading their performances to everyday people sharing funny or interesting clips, YouTube became a vibrant hub for creativity. This content, though often informal and unscripted, resonated deeply with viewers because of its authenticity. The accessibility and relatability of user-generated videos fostered a sense of community that was central to YouTube's early growth.

Companies, too, began to see the platform's potential to reach audiences in new and engaging ways. The success of Nike's Ronaldinho ad was an early example of how businesses could leverage YouTube to amplify their brand messaging. Recognizing the viral power of video, other companies quickly followed suit, uploading promotional content that blended entertainment with marketing. Unlike traditional advertisements, these videos felt less intrusive and more shareable, enabling companies to connect with viewers in a way that felt fresh and innovative.

User-generated content played a critical role in driving YouTube's growth during this period. The platform thrived on the diversity and volume of videos that users contributed, creating a dynamic ecosystem where there was something for everyone. Whether it was quirky skits, heartfelt vlogs, or groundbreaking tutorials, the sheer variety of content attracted a wide range of viewers. Each upload added to the richness of the platform, making it a more appealing destination for both creators and audiences.

What made YouTube particularly unique was its ability to amplify these user-generated creations far beyond what was previously possible. The platform's embedding and sharing features allowed videos to travel across websites, social media, and email, creating a snowball effect of visibility. A single video uploaded by an unknown individual could suddenly be seen by millions, a phenomenon that reinforced YouTube's appeal as a platform where anyone could be discovered.

This interplay between individual creators and companies further accelerated YouTube's growth. As users flocked to the platform to watch and share content, businesses recognized the opportunity to engage with this growing audience. In turn, their investment in creating engaging videos added to YouTube's appeal, drawing even more users and creators into the fold. This virtuous cycle of content creation, sharing, and discovery became the engine of YouTube's early success, setting the stage for its transformation into a global powerhouse.

Chapter 4: The Google Acquisition

YouTube's rapid ascent from a fledgling video-sharing site to a cultural and technological phenomenon was nothing short of remarkable. After its launch in February 2005, the platform quickly gained traction among users. The ease of uploading and sharing videos, combined with the novelty of user-generated content, created a buzz that spread rapidly across the internet. By the end of its first year, YouTube was hosting tens of thousands of videos and receiving millions of daily views, signaling its potential as a major player in the digital space.

Recognizing this momentum, YouTube attracted its first significant financial backing in November 2005. Sequoia Capital, a prominent venture capital firm, invested $3.5 million in the startup, providing the resources necessary to scale the platform. This funding allowed YouTube to upgrade its infrastructure, handle the increasing volume of traffic, and refine its user experience. Sequoia's investment was a vote of confidence in YouTube's vision, and it marked the beginning of a new phase of growth for the company.

By mid-2006, YouTube's popularity had exploded. The platform was hosting over 100 million video views per day, with an ever-growing library of diverse content uploaded by users from around the world. Its success was driven by its ability to tap into a universal human desire: the need to share and connect through storytelling. As more people discovered the platform, it became clear that YouTube was not just a passing trend but a transformative force in the way media was consumed and created.

This rapid growth caught the attention of major technology companies, including Google. At the time, Google was already a dominant force in search and online advertising, but its attempts to create a successful video platform had fallen short.

Recognizing YouTube's potential to complement its ecosystem and expand its reach into the burgeoning online video market, Google made a bold move. In October 2006, Google acquired YouTube for $1.65 billion in stock, making headlines as one of the largest acquisitions in the tech industry at the time.

The acquisition was a turning point for YouTube. Under Google's umbrella, YouTube gained access to the resources and expertise needed to scale its operations further. This included improvements in infrastructure, the introduction of advanced algorithms to recommend content, and the development of monetization tools for creators. For Google, the acquisition was about more than just video; it was an investment in the future of online engagement and a strategic move to solidify its dominance in digital advertising.

The deal was met with excitement and skepticism in equal measure. Supporters saw it as a visionary step, positioning Google at the forefront of the online video revolution. Critics, however, questioned the high valuation and the legal risks associated with hosting copyrighted material. Despite these concerns, the acquisition proved to be a masterstroke. Over time, YouTube evolved into a cornerstone of Google's operations, generating significant revenue and shaping the way people interact with digital content.

In less than two years, YouTube had transformed from a modest startup to a global powerhouse, with Google's acquisition cementing its place in the annals of tech history. It was a testament to the power of a simple idea, executed brilliantly, and it marked the beginning of YouTube's journey to becoming one of the most influential platforms in the world.

The acquisition of YouTube by Google in October 2006 was a moment of triumph for its founders, Chad Hurley, Steve Chen, and Jawed Karim. For three individuals who had started the platform just 20 months earlier in a small office above a pizza shop, the $1.65 billion deal was both a validation of their vision and a recognition of the incredible growth YouTube had achieved in such a short time. It was a watershed moment, not only for them personally but also for the tech industry, signaling the immense value of online video in the evolving digital landscape.

The founders were notably gracious and optimistic in their public reactions. In a heartfelt video message to the YouTube community, Hurley and Chen expressed their gratitude to the users and creators who had made the platform what it was. They emphasized that YouTube's success was a shared achievement, rooted in the vibrant content and engagement of its community. This sense of humility and collaboration underscored the ethos that had driven YouTube's growth: a belief in empowering individuals to share their stories with the world.

For the founders, the acquisition represented not an end but a new beginning. They viewed Google's involvement as an opportunity to take YouTube to the next level, leveraging the resources and expertise of one of the most powerful companies in the tech world. Google's infrastructure would allow YouTube to handle its explosive growth more effectively, while its leadership in search and advertising technology promised to unlock new ways for the platform to serve its creators and audiences.

From Google's perspective, the acquisition was about much more than simply owning a popular website. Google's executives, including CEO Eric Schmidt, saw YouTube as the next frontier in online engagement. They envisioned a platform that could revolutionize media consumption by making video content as searchable, accessible, and shareable as the web itself. For Google, YouTube was not just a video-sharing site; it was a vehicle for transforming how people interacted with media, from entertainment and education to news and beyond.

At the heart of Google's vision was the idea of creating a seamless ecosystem where users could discover and consume video content effortlessly. This meant investing in cutting-edge algorithms to recommend videos tailored to users' interests, refining the platform's interface for ease of use, and integrating advertising in ways that benefited both creators and the company. Google also aimed to address YouTube's challenges, including copyright concerns, by introducing tools that would help protect intellectual property while maintaining the platform's openness.

The acquisition was a bold bet on the future, and both the founders and Google were aligned in their belief that YouTube had only scratched the surface of its potential. Together, they would embark on a journey to transform YouTube from a groundbreaking startup into a cultural and technological institution, reshaping the way the world shared and experienced video content. The deal marked the beginning of a new era for YouTube, one where its possibilities seemed as vast as the internet itself.

Chapter 5: Building a Platform for Everyone

In 2007, YouTube took a groundbreaking step that would forever alter the dynamics of online content creation by launching the YouTube Partner Program. This initiative introduced a monetization system, allowing creators to earn revenue from the videos they uploaded. For the first time, everyday users could turn their hobbies and creative passions into a source of income, marking a significant shift in how content was valued and incentivized in the digital age.

The concept was simple but revolutionary. By integrating advertisements into videos and sharing the revenue with creators, YouTube provided a financial incentive for users to produce high-quality content and build loyal audiences. This arrangement democratized the media landscape, giving individuals from all walks of life an opportunity to participate in and benefit from the burgeoning creator economy. Creators who had once shared videos purely for fun or self-expression suddenly found themselves at the forefront of a new and potentially lucrative industry.

The impact of the Partner Program was immediate and profound. It spurred an explosion of creativity on the platform, as aspiring filmmakers, musicians, educators, and entertainers flocked to YouTube with dreams of turning their ideas into thriving channels. The promise of monetization motivated creators to refine their craft, invest in better equipment, and engage more deeply with their audiences. It also transformed YouTube into a platform that wasn't just a repository for videos but a vibrant ecosystem of innovation and storytelling.

For many, the Partner Program was life-changing. Creators who gained traction on the platform began earning significant incomes, with some achieving six-figure revenues within a year. This newfound financial freedom enabled them to pursue their passions full-time, blurring the lines between amateur and professional content production. It also gave rise to a new type of celebrity—the YouTube star—whose influence extended far beyond the platform into mainstream culture.

The program also had a ripple effect on YouTube's growth and reputation. As more creators joined the platform and produced diverse, engaging content, YouTube became a go-to destination for audiences seeking everything from entertainment and education to niche interests. The sheer variety and quality of videos attracted advertisers, who were eager to tap into YouTube's growing audience. This influx of advertising revenue further fueled the platform's expansion, creating a virtuous cycle of growth that benefited creators, viewers, and YouTube itself.

The YouTube Partner Program was more than just a monetization tool—it was a paradigm shift that redefined how content creators interacted with their audiences and the broader media industry. By empowering individuals to profit from their creativity, YouTube set the stage for the creator economy we know today, fostering a culture where anyone with a camera and an idea could potentially reach—and impact—the world. It was a bold move that not only elevated the platform but also cemented its role as a trailblazer in the evolution of digital media.

In 2007, YouTube introduced advertisements to its platform, a move that marked the beginning of its monetization model. This shift allowed YouTube to generate revenue while sharing the profits with content creators through the newly launched Partner Program. Advertisements, whether displayed before, during, or alongside videos, became a core part of YouTube's ecosystem, helping to sustain the platform's rapid growth and incentivize creators to produce engaging content.

This model was groundbreaking for its time, as it created a mutually beneficial relationship between YouTube, advertisers, and creators. Advertisers gained access to a diverse and global audience, while creators were rewarded financially for their work. For YouTube, the ad-based system provided the resources needed to invest in the platform's infrastructure and innovation. This monetization framework quickly became a cornerstone of the platform, transforming YouTube from a startup into a revenue-generating powerhouse.

As YouTube grew, so did the expectations of its users. Recognizing the need to enhance the user experience, YouTube continuously evolved its interface and introduced new features. These changes not only improved usability but also catered to the needs of both creators and viewers, solidifying YouTube's position as the leading video-sharing platform.

One of the most significant advancements was the introduction of high-definition (HD) video support in 2008. As internet speeds improved and audiences demanded better quality, YouTube adapted by allowing creators to upload videos in

720p and later 1080p. This upgrade was a turning point, as it bridged the gap between amateur and professional content. HD videos made the platform more appealing to filmmakers, musicians, and businesses, elevating the overall quality of content and attracting a broader audience.

Another key milestone was the launch of live streaming. Initially rolled out in 2011 for select events, live streaming allowed creators to broadcast content in real time, connecting with audiences in ways that pre-recorded videos couldn't match. From concerts and sports events to personal vlogs and interactive Q&A sessions, live streaming opened new possibilities for engagement and immediacy. It also positioned YouTube as a competitor to traditional broadcast media, giving viewers access to real-time content on a global scale.

Beyond these major updates, YouTube introduced a host of features designed to enhance user interaction and content discovery. Playlists, annotations, and personalized recommendations made it easier for viewers to find and enjoy videos tailored to their interests. The introduction of mobile apps ensured that users could access YouTube anytime, anywhere, further cementing its dominance in the digital media landscape.

Through these innovations, YouTube transformed itself into more than just a video-sharing platform. It became a dynamic and adaptable ecosystem that continuously pushed the boundaries of what was possible in digital media. The combination of advertisements, monetization, HD support, and live streaming solidified YouTube's reputation as a trailblazer, setting new standards for how people create, share, and experience video content in the modern era.

Chapter 6: The Global Phenomenon

YouTube's meteoric rise transformed it into a platform of staggering global influence, with statistics that underscore its unparalleled reach and impact. From its modest beginnings, YouTube quickly became a cornerstone of digital culture, amassing a user base that spans nearly every country and demographic on Earth.

The platform's audience is vast and continuously growing, with over 2 billion logged-in monthly users as of recent years. This figure represents just a portion of its actual reach, as countless viewers access content without signing in. YouTube's accessibility across devices—whether on desktop, mobile, or smart TVs—has made it a universal platform, catering to users of all ages, interests, and geographies.

The scale of engagement on YouTube is equally impressive. Users collectively watch over 1 billion hours of video daily, consuming content that ranges from educational tutorials and entertainment to news and personal vlogs. This level of watch time reflects YouTube's ability to cater to a diverse array of preferences, ensuring that there is truly something for everyone. The platform's algorithm plays a significant role here, delivering personalized recommendations that keep viewers engaged and exploring.

When it comes to content creation, YouTube's growth has been nothing short of explosive. Over 500 hours of video are uploaded every minute, resulting in a library of content that expands exponentially by the second. This flood of user-generated videos has made YouTube the largest repository of visual content in history, offering an endless stream of ideas, stories, and perspectives. It also reflects the democratization of media, where anyone with a camera and internet access can contribute to the global conversation.

YouTube's global reach is further highlighted by the fact that more than 80% of its views come from outside the United States. The platform's localization efforts, which include support for over 100 languages and tailored regional content, have been instrumental in achieving this level of international success. It has become a cultural melting pot, where creators and audiences from all corners of the world connect and share their experiences.

These statistics only scratch the surface of YouTube's impact. Beyond numbers, the platform's ability to shape cultural trends, amplify voices, and create economic opportunities is unparalleled. Its reach is not just about scale but also about depth—connecting people, ideas, and communities in ways that were unimaginable before its existence. As these figures continue to grow, so does

YouTube's influence as a global force in the digital age.

YouTube's international adoption was one of the driving forces behind its transformation from a U.S.-based startup to a truly global phenomenon. Recognizing early on that the platform's potential extended far beyond its home market, YouTube implemented strategies to cater to users worldwide, tailoring its features and content to suit the needs of diverse regions and cultures.

Localization was key to YouTube's global success. The platform launched region-specific versions in dozens of countries, offering translated interfaces, tailored recommendations, and curated trending pages to reflect local interests. This approach made YouTube more accessible and relevant to users across the globe, from bustling urban centers to remote rural areas. By supporting over 100 languages, YouTube ensured that it could serve as a universal platform where people could share and consume content in their native tongues.

Beyond language, YouTube adapted its tools to empower creators in different regions. Monetization options, content guidelines, and community initiatives were refined to align with local regulations and cultural norms. This inclusivity encouraged creators from all corners of the world to join the platform, further enriching its diversity. Whether it was cooking tutorials from India, music videos from Brazil, or comedy skits from South Korea, YouTube became a melting pot of cultures and creativity, connecting people in unprecedented ways.

Throughout its evolution, iconic creators and viral moments played a pivotal role in shaping YouTube's culture. These milestones showcased the platform's ability to amplify talent and bring communities together. One early example was the rise of *Charlie Bit My Finger*, a humorous home video featuring two young brothers from the United Kingdom. This clip, which became one of the most-watched videos on the platform, exemplified the charm of everyday moments and how they could resonate globally.

Creators like PewDiePie, a Swedish gamer, demonstrated how YouTube could turn individuals into global superstars. Starting with simple gaming commentary, PewDiePie built a massive fanbase, becoming the most-subscribed individual creator for several years. His success highlighted YouTube's unique ability to cater to niche interests while fostering deep connections between creators and their audiences.

Viral phenomena like *Gangnam Style* by South Korean artist Psy further underscored YouTube's power as a global cultural hub. The music video's playful choreography and catchy tune captured hearts worldwide, breaking records as the first video to surpass 1 billion views. Moments like this cemented YouTube's role as a platform where international trends could originate and thrive.

Educational creators also contributed to the platform's identity. Channels like India's *Study IQ* or the globally renowned *CrashCourse* demonstrated YouTube's potential as a tool for learning and empowerment. By offering free access to knowledge on virtually any topic, these creators expanded the platform's purpose beyond entertainment to include education and skill-building.

These examples, along with countless others, illustrate how YouTube has become a reflection of the world's diversity and dynamism. Its international adoption and localized strategies, combined with the creative contributions of its users, have shaped a culture that celebrates both individuality and global connection. In doing so, YouTube has redefined what it means to share stories, create community, and inspire change on a global scale.

Chapter 7: Shaping Media and History

YouTube's impact extends far beyond entertainment and education; it has played a pivotal role in shaping history, serving as a platform for activism, political discourse, and societal change. The platform's ability to amplify voices and disseminate information rapidly became particularly evident during the 2011 Arab Spring and in political events like presidential debates. These moments demonstrated how YouTube could transcend its role as a video-sharing site to become a powerful tool for advocacy and engagement.

During the Arab Spring, a series of pro-democracy uprisings across the Middle East and North Africa, YouTube emerged as an essential medium for documenting and sharing the realities on the ground. Activists and ordinary citizens used the platform to upload videos of protests, government crackdowns, and public demonstrations, often in real-time. These clips provided an unfiltered view of events that traditional media outlets could not always capture, offering the world a firsthand account of the struggles and aspirations of millions.

YouTube's global reach enabled these videos to bypass state-controlled media and censorship, bringing international attention to the movements. They were shared widely on social media platforms, fueling solidarity and support from people around the world. The platform also gave activists a way to coordinate efforts and inspire others to join the cause, becoming a digital megaphone for freedom and democracy. The raw, often harrowing footage uploaded during the Arab Spring underscored YouTube's potential as a tool for transparency and change.

In the realm of politics, YouTube similarly transformed the way political discourse unfolded. A notable example came during the 2007 and 2008 U.S. presidential campaigns, when candidates began using the platform to announce their candidacies and connect with voters. For the first time, YouTube allowed politicians to speak directly to the public without the filter of traditional media, creating a more personal and interactive form of communication.

In 2007, YouTube partnered with CNN to host the first-ever presidential debate driven by user-generated questions. Citizens from across the country submitted video questions, which were played during the live debate and addressed by the candidates. This format democratized the debate process, giving everyday people a voice in shaping the political conversation. It was a groundbreaking moment that highlighted YouTube's role in fostering civic engagement and bringing voters closer to the electoral process.

The platform's influence on politics and activism continued to grow, with live streams of major events, policy announcements, and even protests becoming a staple of its content. From rallying movements for social justice to providing a stage for grassroots campaigns, YouTube proved to be a catalyst for participation and change.

These historic moments, whether in the streets of Cairo or on the debate stages of the United States, illustrate how YouTube has evolved into a platform with profound societal implications. Its ability to amplify marginalized voices, challenge the status quo, and connect people across borders has made it an indispensable tool in shaping the course of modern history.

YouTube's emergence as a transformative platform can be likened to earlier media revolutions, such as the advent of television in the mid-20th century. Just as television reshaped communication, entertainment, and culture by bringing visual storytelling into homes worldwide, YouTube revolutionized media by democratizing both content creation and distribution. However, YouTube's impact goes even further, leveraging the interactivity and accessibility of the internet to reach unprecedented levels of influence in global politics, culture, and education.

Television, in its time, was groundbreaking for its ability to create a shared cultural experience. Iconic moments—such as the moon landing or the televised debates between John F. Kennedy and Richard Nixon—shaped collective memory and demonstrated the power of visual media to inform and unify. Yet, television was a one-way medium, controlled by a few broadcasters who determined what the public consumed. YouTube broke this mold by turning the audience into creators, empowering individuals to share their own stories and perspectives.

Unlike television's top-down approach, YouTube operates on a bottom-up model, where anyone with an internet connection can contribute to the global conversation. This democratization of content has led to a diverse and vibrant media landscape, where voices from marginalized communities and remote regions can gain visibility. While television brought stories to the masses, YouTube gave the masses the tools to tell their own stories, fundamentally altering the dynamics of media power and influence.

One of YouTube's most profound areas of impact is global politics. The platform has become a powerful tool for activism, campaigning, and awareness. From live-streamed protests to candid political speeches, YouTube provides an unfiltered window into the events that shape the world. It has been used to expose corruption, mobilize movements, and rally support for causes that might otherwise go unnoticed. Politicians and organizations leverage YouTube to communicate directly with their audiences, bypassing traditional media gatekeepers and fostering a more engaged electorate.

Culturally, YouTube has redefined what it means to consume and create media. It has blurred the lines between professional and amateur content, making room for independent creators to become influential figures. Trends that once originated in studios or editorial rooms now emerge from bedrooms and small-scale productions, giving rise to viral challenges, music sensations, and innovative storytelling formats. YouTube has become a global stage for creativity, shaping the zeitgeist and connecting cultures in ways that were previously unimaginable.

In education, YouTube's contributions are unparalleled. The platform has become a global classroom, offering free access to knowledge on virtually any subject. Channels like Khan Academy, CrashCourse, and TED-Ed have revolutionized learning, providing high-quality educational content to millions. Whether it's students seeking help with homework, professionals honing their skills, or lifelong learners exploring new interests, YouTube has made education more accessible and personalized than ever before.

The platform's influence also extends to how we process information. Unlike television, which relies on passive consumption, YouTube encourages active engagement. Viewers can comment, share, and interact with creators, fostering a sense of community and dialogue. This interactivity has reshaped not just how content is consumed, but also how it is created and refined in response to audience feedback.

In essence, YouTube represents the next evolution of media, building on the legacy of television while surpassing its limitations. Its influence on politics, culture, and education has not only changed the way we consume media but also the way we understand and engage with the world. It is a revolution rooted in participation, diversity, and connection, embodying the full potential of the digital age.

Chapter 8: The Cultural Zeitgeist

YouTube has become a breeding ground for innovative forms of infotainment, where creators merge education with entertainment to captivate audiences while delivering knowledge. This hybrid approach has redefined how people learn and engage with complex topics, giving rise to channels that have become pillars of this new genre. Among them, Vsauce and CrashCourse stand out as pioneers, showcasing the platform's potential to make learning accessible, engaging, and even thrilling.

Vsauce, created by Michael Stevens in 2010, has revolutionized the way science, philosophy, and curiosity-driven exploration are presented online. With its signature format—blending thought-provoking questions, deep dives into scientific concepts, and quirky humor—Vsauce has captured the imaginations of millions. Episodes tackle everything from the nature of infinity to the science of illusions, often weaving seemingly unrelated topics into a cohesive and enlightening narrative. Stevens' ability to present complex ideas in a digestible and entertaining manner has made Vsauce a go-to channel for curious minds, proving that education doesn't have to be dry or formal to be impactful.

CrashCourse, founded by brothers Hank and John Green in 2012, is another trailblazer in the infotainment space. The channel offers a series of educational videos covering a wide range of subjects, from history and literature to physics and economics. Each series is meticulously crafted, with vibrant animations, engaging scripts, and a clear pedagogical structure that appeals to learners of all ages. CrashCourse has become an invaluable resource for students and educators alike, demonstrating how high-quality content can bridge gaps in traditional education systems. Its ability to condense complex subjects into concise, entertaining lessons has earned it widespread acclaim and millions of dedicated viewers.

These channels exemplify a broader trend on YouTube, where creators use the platform's versatility to reimagine educational content. They cater to the curiosity of a global audience, breaking down barriers of access, cost, and traditional classroom constraints. The success of Vsauce, CrashCourse, and similar channels underscores a shift in how people seek and consume knowledge. Instead of relying solely on formal institutions, learners now turn to YouTube for dynamic, on-demand education that fits into their lives.

What sets these channels apart is their ability to connect with viewers on a personal level. The creators often address their audience directly, fostering a sense of community and shared curiosity. This interactive approach, combined with the visual and narrative techniques of modern storytelling, keeps viewers engaged and inspired.

The result is content that not only informs but also encourages critical thinking and lifelong learning.

The impact of these channels extends beyond individual viewers. They have influenced the educational landscape, inspiring a new generation of creators to explore similar formats and pushing traditional institutions to rethink how they deliver knowledge in the digital age. Through their innovative approach, Vsauce, CrashCourse, and their counterparts have redefined what it means to learn, proving that education and entertainment are not mutually exclusive but can thrive together in the digital era.

YouTube's evolution gave rise to a vibrant array of niche genres, each thriving within its ecosystem and redefining the way audiences consume entertainment. Comedy, pranks, music, and special effects became some of the most popular categories, showcasing the platform's ability to cater to diverse tastes and interests. These genres not only captured massive viewership but also created entirely new avenues for creative expression, challenging traditional media norms and fostering the emergence of a new type of celebrity.

Comedy found a natural home on YouTube, with creators using the platform to experiment with sketches, parodies, and improvisation. Channels like *Smosh* and *Nigahiga* were among the early pioneers, delivering short, humorous videos that quickly gained massive followings. Unlike traditional television or stand-up comedy, these creators had complete creative freedom, which allowed them to connect with audiences in a more personal and relatable way. This genre thrived on spontaneity and authenticity, with many creators drawing humor from everyday situations, cultural observations, and internet trends.

The prank genre also flourished, appealing to audiences with its mix of shock value, humor, and unpredictability. Channels such as *VitalyzdTv* and *FouseyTube* became well-known for elaborate stunts that ranged from lighthearted pranks to provocative social experiments. While this genre occasionally sparked controversy over ethical boundaries, it showcased the platform's ability to push creative limits and engage viewers in real-time interactions.

Music became another cornerstone of YouTube's identity, revolutionizing the way artists reached audiences. Aspiring musicians, such as Justin Bieber, found their big break on the platform, using it as a stage to showcase their talent and connect directly with fans. Established artists also embraced YouTube, leveraging its global reach to release music videos and live performances. Additionally, cover artists and independent musicians like *Boyce Avenue* and *Lindsey Stirling* cultivated dedicated fanbases, proving that YouTube could launch careers without the traditional backing of record labels.

Special effects-driven content emerged as a testament to the platform's creative potential. Channels like *Corridor Digital* and *Freddie Wong* brought cinematic-quality effects to YouTube, delivering short films and action-packed sequences that rivaled Hollywood productions. These creators demonstrated that, with the right skills and tools, high-quality storytelling was achievable on a budget. Their success inspired countless others to experiment with visual effects, expanding the boundaries of what could be accomplished by independent creators.

The rise of these niche genres coincided with the emergence of YouTube celebrities—individuals who gained fame and influence entirely through their presence on the platform. Unlike traditional celebrities, YouTube stars often built their audiences through direct engagement and authenticity, creating a sense of intimacy and relatability that resonated with viewers. This new breed of celebrity included gamers like *PewDiePie*, beauty gurus like *Michelle Phan*, and vloggers like *Zoella*, each of whom amassed millions of followers and became household names.

The impact of YouTube celebrities extended far beyond the platform, disrupting traditional media's dominance. Brands began partnering with YouTube influencers for endorsements, recognizing their unparalleled ability to connect with younger, tech-savvy audiences. Traditional media outlets also took notice, with YouTube stars appearing in movies, television shows, and even creating their own mainstream ventures.

The shift in audience attention toward YouTube personalities forced traditional media to adapt. Networks and studios began exploring digital-first content, while advertisers shifted budgets to include influencer campaigns and online ads. YouTube's ability to empower creators, foster niche genres, and cultivate authentic connections reshaped the entertainment landscape, proving that the future of media belonged not just to institutions but to individuals willing to share their creativity with the world.

Chapter 9: Challenges and Controversies

As YouTube grew into a global media powerhouse, it faced complex challenges that came with its scale and influence. Among these were issues related to copyright, misinformation, and content moderation. Balancing freedom of expression with responsible platform management became a delicate tightrope act, one that sparked ongoing debates about YouTube's role in shaping digital culture. Adding to these challenges were criticisms of the platform's algorithms, advertising policies, and their impact on creators, highlighting tensions between innovation, ethics, and accountability.

One of the earliest and most persistent issues YouTube encountered was copyright infringement. With thousands of videos being uploaded every minute, policing unauthorized use of copyrighted material proved daunting. Content owners frequently discovered their music, movies, or shows re-uploaded without permission, prompting legal battles and takedown requests. In response, YouTube developed the Content ID system, an automated tool that allowed rights holders to identify and manage their intellectual property on the platform. While Content ID offered a solution for detecting violations, it also faced criticism for being overly rigid, sometimes flagging legitimate content, such as parodies or educational material, under the broad scope of copyright law.

Misinformation emerged as another critical issue, particularly as YouTube became a primary source of news and information for millions. The platform's open nature, which allowed anyone to share their views, also made it a breeding ground for conspiracy theories, false claims, and misleading content. This was especially evident during major events like elections and public health crises, where misinformation could spread rapidly, influencing public opinion and behavior. YouTube implemented policies to limit the reach of harmful content, such as removing videos that violated community guidelines and promoting authoritative sources. However, critics argued that these measures often fell short, with problematic content remaining accessible or reappearing in different forms.

Content moderation, in general, became a contentious topic. YouTube's efforts to enforce its guidelines often led to accusations of censorship, with creators and viewers questioning where the line should be drawn between free expression and harmful speech. The platform walked a fine line, attempting to uphold its commitment to open dialogue while preventing abuse, harassment, and the spread of dangerous ideas. Automated moderation systems, though efficient at scale, were frequently criticized for making errors, such as demonetizing or removing videos that did not actually violate policies.

The role of YouTube's algorithms added another layer of complexity. Designed to recommend content and keep viewers engaged, these algorithms were often blamed for creating "filter bubbles" or amplifying extreme content to maximize watch time. Critics argued that the algorithms prioritized sensationalism over substance, inadvertently promoting divisive or harmful material. For creators, the opaque nature of these algorithms created uncertainty, as minor changes in the recommendation system could drastically affect their visibility and income.

YouTube's advertising model also faced scrutiny, both from creators and advertisers. The platform's reliance on ad revenue meant that advertisers sought to distance themselves from controversial content, leading to the "adpocalypse"—a period when many videos were demonetized due to stricter ad suitability guidelines. This shift disproportionately affected smaller creators, who relied on ad revenue to sustain their channels. The balance between satisfying advertisers, supporting creators, and maintaining user trust proved to be a persistent challenge.

Despite these issues, YouTube continued to evolve its policies and practices, striving to address concerns while preserving the openness that defined its identity. Initiatives like expanded transparency reports, improved Content ID processes, and partnerships with fact-checking organizations reflected its commitment to accountability. However, the ongoing criticisms underscored the inherent difficulties of managing a platform as vast and diverse as YouTube.

Ultimately, these challenges highlight the dual-edged nature of YouTube's influence. As a platform that champions creativity and expression, it must also bear the responsibility of fostering a safe, ethical, and balanced environment. The ongoing dialogue between creators, viewers, and the platform itself is a testament to YouTube's complex role in shaping the digital age.

Chapter 10: YouTube Today and Tomorrow

YouTube has grown into a digital giant, with billions of users logging in each month to watch, share, and create content. As of today, it stands as the second most-visited website in the world, surpassed only by its parent company, Google. This immense scale makes YouTube an integral part of the digital ecosystem, influencing everything from media consumption habits to advertising strategies. It is not just a platform but a cultural and technological phenomenon that has redefined how the world connects and communicates.

The platform's reach extends far beyond casual entertainment. Its user base spans every demographic, offering content in countless languages and catering to virtually every interest imaginable. With over 500 hours of video uploaded every minute and over 1 billion hours of content consumed daily, YouTube has become a cornerstone of the internet, hosting the largest repository of visual content in human history. Its role in shaping digital culture is unmatched, as it serves as both a stage for emerging talent and a library of knowledge, creativity, and innovation.

One of YouTube's most transformative impacts has been its role in replacing traditional television. As audiences increasingly shift toward on-demand, personalized content, YouTube has positioned itself as the modern alternative to linear TV. Unlike traditional broadcasting, YouTube offers unparalleled interactivity, enabling viewers to engage with content through comments, shares, and likes. Live streaming, premium channels, and original content have further blurred the lines between YouTube and conventional television networks. For younger generations, YouTube is not just a supplement to TV—it is the primary medium for video consumption.

This shift has also transformed the advertising landscape. Advertisers who once relied on TV commercials to reach audiences are now turning to YouTube for its precision targeting and measurable impact. The platform's ability to deliver ads tailored to individual preferences, combined with its vast reach, has made it a cornerstone of modern marketing strategies. Programs like Google Preferred, which allows advertisers to place their messages on premium channels, highlight how YouTube has redefined what it means to advertise effectively in the digital age. The rise of influencer marketing, driven by YouTube's creator economy, further underscores this trend, as brands collaborate with creators to deliver authentic, relatable campaigns.

As YouTube continues to grow, its future is a topic of both excitement and speculation. On the innovation front, advancements in artificial intelligence and machine learning are expected to enhance the platform's capabilities, from more accurate content recommendations to improved moderation systems. Virtual reality (VR) and augmented reality (AR) are also poised to play a significant role, potentially transforming how users interact with content and creators. Features like 360-degree videos and immersive experiences hint at a future where YouTube becomes a pioneer in next-generation media.

However, challenges remain. Issues such as misinformation, content moderation, and the balance between freedom of expression and platform responsibility will continue to demand attention. Creators also face uncertainty regarding algorithm changes and monetization policies, which can impact their livelihoods. Competition from other platforms, such as TikTok and emerging streaming services, adds pressure for YouTube to innovate while maintaining its core identity.

Despite these hurdles, YouTube's growth potential remains immense. Its adaptability, global reach, and commitment to empowering creators position it as a key player in the evolving digital landscape. As technology advances and user expectations shift, YouTube is likely to remain at the forefront, shaping the future of media and redefining how the world shares, learns, and entertains itself.

In essence, YouTube has become far more than a video-sharing platform—it is a reflection of the digital age's possibilities and complexities. Its journey from a small startup to a global powerhouse is a testament to the power of creativity, innovation, and connection. As it continues to evolve, YouTube will undoubtedly remain a central force in the ongoing transformation of how humanity consumes and interacts with media.

Conclusion

YouTube's journey from a modest idea conceived by three friends to a global phenomenon is a testament to the transformative power of creativity and vision. Chad Hurley, Steve Chen, and Jawed Karim began with a simple goal: to create a platform where people could share videos effortlessly. What they built, however, was far more than a website—it was a revolution in how humanity communicates, connects, and consumes media.

Their creation reshaped the very fabric of modern culture, empowering individuals to express themselves, share their stories, and reach audiences on an unprecedented scale. YouTube broke down the barriers of traditional media, allowing anyone with an idea and a camera to become a creator, a teacher, or even a global sensation. It democratized content creation, giving a voice to the voiceless and creating a platform where diversity, creativity, and innovation could thrive.

Over the years, YouTube has proven to be far more than a technological achievement. It is a cultural force that has influenced global politics, education, and entertainment, bridging gaps and fostering connections across borders. From shaping movements like the Arab Spring to introducing new forms of infotainment and launching careers, YouTube has become embedded in the fabric of daily life. Its enduring significance lies in its ability to adapt and evolve while remaining true to its core purpose: to provide a space where ideas and experiences can be shared freely.

As we reflect on YouTube's journey, it is impossible to overlook its place in history. Much like the advent of the printing press, radio, or television, YouTube represents a milestone in human communication. It has not only changed how content is created and consumed but also redefined how people relate to one another in an increasingly digital world. Whether through a viral video, an educational series, or a live stream connecting millions, YouTube has become a platform where moments are made and shared in real time, leaving an indelible mark on the 21st century.

As it continues to grow and adapt to new challenges and opportunities, YouTube remains a symbol of what is possible when technology and creativity converge. Its story is one of innovation, resilience, and the universal human desire to connect and communicate. It stands as a reminder that even the simplest ideas, when pursued with passion and purpose, can change the world in ways no one could have imagined.

Made in United States
Orlando, FL
13 April 2025